EYE OPENERS

Arts & Crafts

**BLACKBIRCH®
PRESS**

THOMSON
GALE

San Diego • Detroit • New York • San Francisco • Cleveland
New Haven, Conn. • Waterville, Maine • London • Munich

LIBRARY OF CONGRESS CATALOGING-IN-PUBLICATION DATA

Nathan, Emma.
  Arts & Crafts / by Emma Nathan.
    p. cm. — (Eyeopeners series)
  Includes index.
  Summary: Introduces some of the crafts indigenous to various countries throughout the world, including Javanese shadow puppets from Indonesia and Chinese calligraphy.
  ISBN 1-56711-598-5 (alk. paper)
  1. Handicraft—History—Juvenile literature. [1. Handicraft.] I. Title. II. Series: Nathan, Emma. Emma. Eyeopeners series.
TT15 .N38 2003
745—dc21   2002014080

Printed in United States
10 9 8 7 6 5 4 3 2 1

TABLE OF CONTENTS

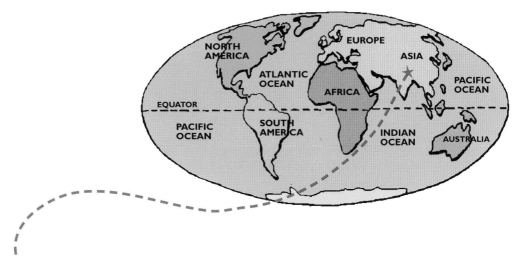

NEPAL (nuh-PAHL)

Nepal is on the continent of Asia. It is a small country between India and China.

People in Nepal make masks for festivals and celebrations.

The masks are made from papier-mâché (pay-per-muh-SHAY).

Some masks are hung on a wall to protect a home from evil spirits.

◀ Masks

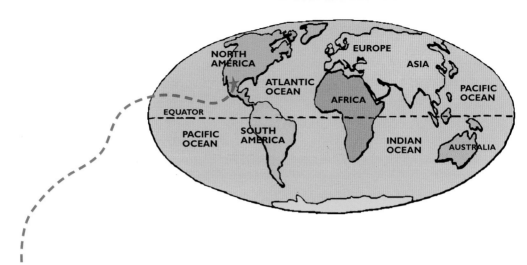

MEXICO (MEKKS-ih-ko)

Mexico is on the continent of North America.

People have been making pottery in Mexico since ancient times.

Mexico's clay soil is good for making pottery.

Some of Mexico's clay is orange and some is red.

One city in Mexico is famous for its black clay.

◄ Pottery

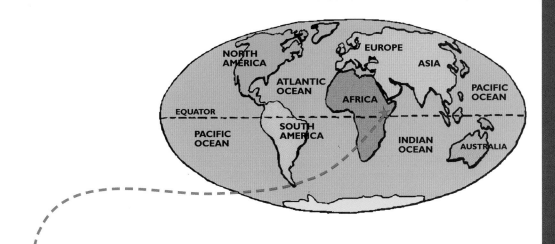

KENYA (KEN-yuh)

Kenya is on the continent of Africa.

Some of the native people of Kenya are called the Masai (muh-SY).

Masai women make jewelry.

The women make bracelets, necklaces, and other jewelry with beads.

Masai men and women wear beaded earrings in their ears.

◀ **Necklace**

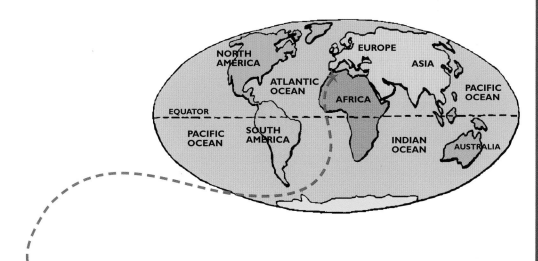

MOROCCO (maw-ROCK-o)

Morocco is on the continent of Africa.

Morocco is in north Africa.

Most people in Morocco are Muslims.

Muslims have a tradition of making very beautiful tile mosaics (moh-ZAY-icks).

The city of Fez is famous for especially beautiful mosaics.

◀ **Mosaic fountain**

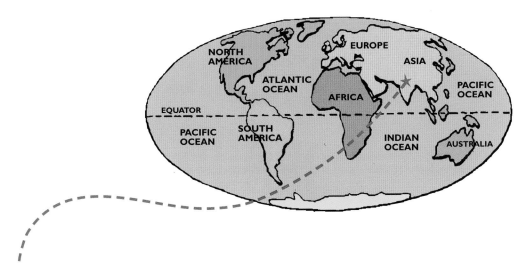

INDIA (IN-dee-ya)

India is on the continent of Asia.

Henna decoration is the art of body painting in India.

Henna is a special dye. It is used to draw beautiful patterns and designs on the skin.

When women in India get married, they have special henna patterns painted on their hands and feet.

◀ **Henna designs**

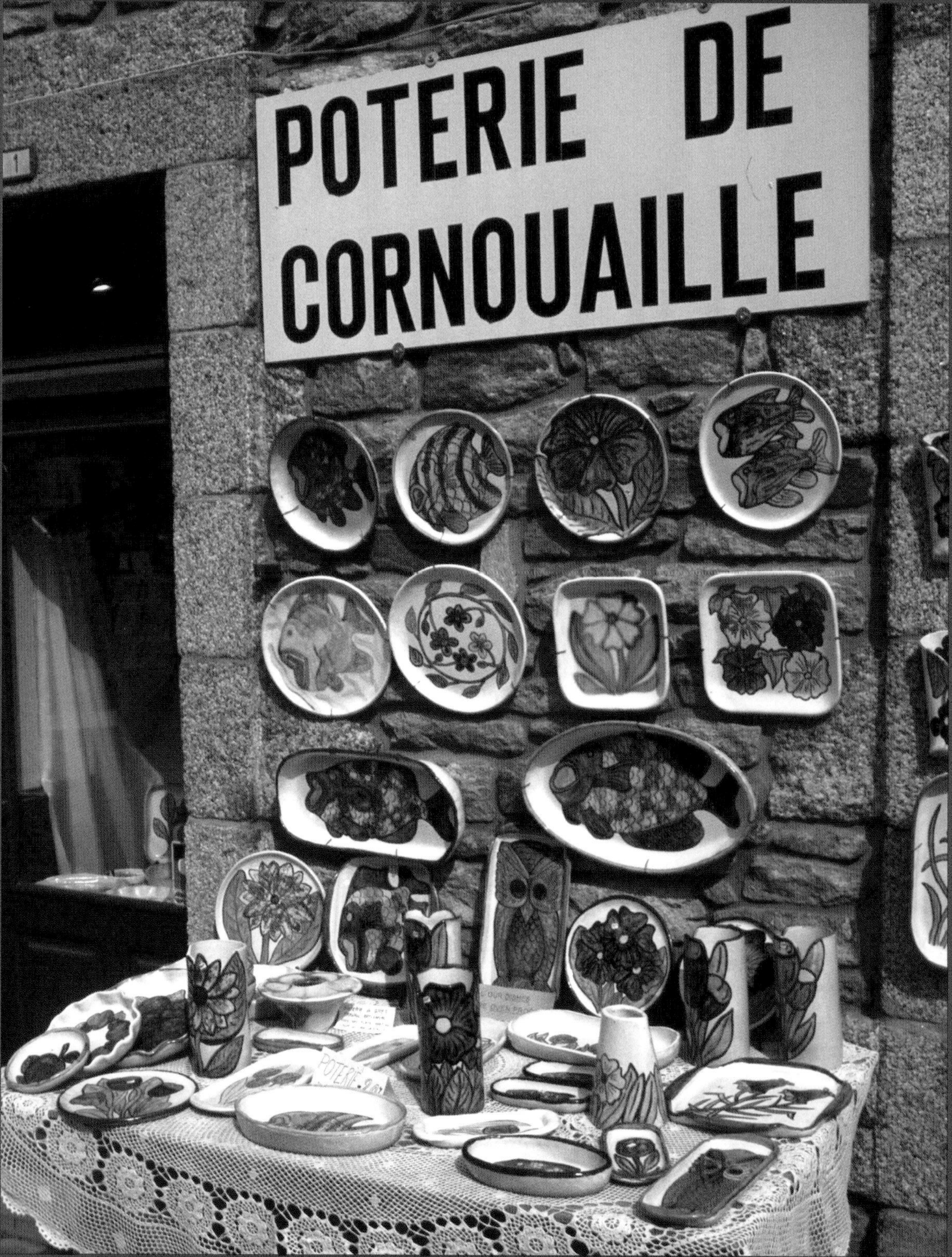
POTERIE DE
CORNOUAILLE

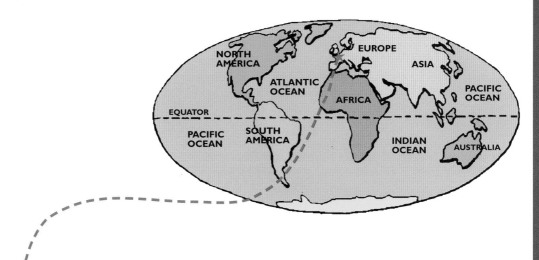

FRANCE (frants)

France is on the continent of Europe.

France is famous for its fine porcelain (POR-suh-linn) pottery.

Porcelain is the hardest kind of ceramic.

Porcelain is made to let light flow through it.

Fine porcelain is most often used for fancy china and statues.

◀ **Pottery**

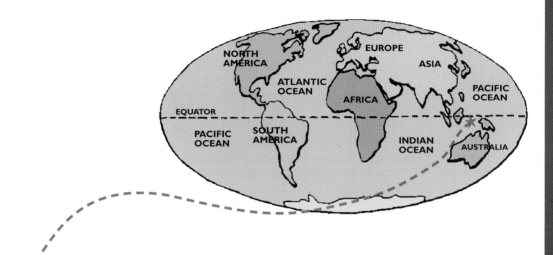

INDONESIA (in-doe-NEE-zhuh)

Indonesia is part of Asia.

Indonesia is a nation of more than 13,500 islands.

One of the biggest islands in Indonesia is Java.

On Java, special puppets are made for a special puppet show.

The puppets perform behind a screen so only their shadows are seen.

◀ **Puppets**

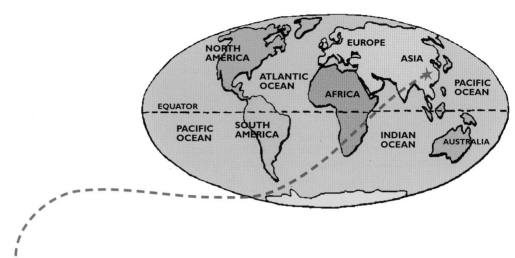

CHINA (CHY-nuh)

China is on the continent of Asia.

One of China's oldest arts is a kind of painting called calligraphy (kuh-LIH-gra-fee).

Calligraphy is the art of writing words.

Chinese artists use a brush called a *pi*. They dip the brush in ink called *mo*.

Most artists paint on rice paper or silk.

◀ **Calligraphy**

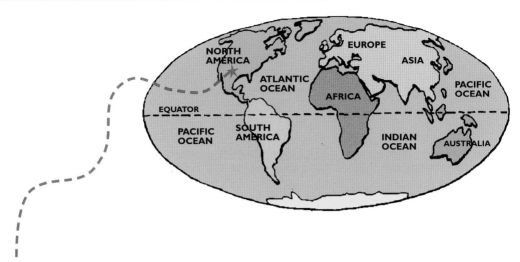

UNITED STATES (yu-nye-ted STAYTS)

The United States is on the continent of North America.

Many groups of Native Americans live in the United States.

One group of Native Americans is the Navajo (NAH-vuh-hoe).

The Navajo are famous for weaving blankets and rugs.

Navajo blankets and rugs have beautiful patterns and colors. Many are made from sheep's wool.

◀ **Weaving a Navajo blanket**

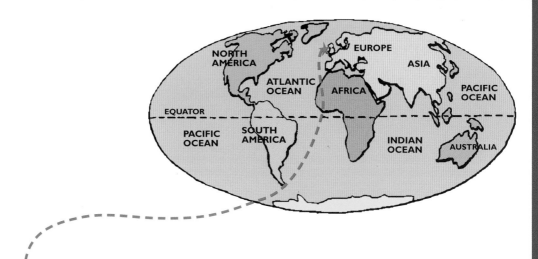

IRELAND (EYE-er-lind)

Ireland is part of the continent of Europe.

Ireland is an island nation with many green hills and pastures.

Sheep are found all over Ireland. They provide wool to people who weave.

Irish wool is famous around the world. Many people buy socks, hats, and sweaters made from Irish wool.

◀ **Spinning wool to weave**

Index

For More Information

Websites

Arts-n-Crafts
http://www.rainfall.com/crafts

The Metropolitan Museum of Art
http://www.metmuseum.org

Worldwide Wheat Weavers
http://www.geocities.com/Heartland/Plains/4565

Books

Braman, Arlette N. *Kids Around the World Create! The Best Crafts and Activities from Many Lands. New York:* John Wiley & Sons, 1999.

Stull, Katherine. *Hands on Crafts for Kids: Crafts Around the World.* Katherine A. Stull, Inc., 1998.

Terzian, Alexandra M. *The Kids' Multicultural Art Book: Art & Craft Experiences from Around the World. Charlotte, VT:* Williamson Publishing, 1993.